Manifest Your Best You

A guided workbook

Cheryl Ann Hunter

TABLE OF CONTENTS

Contents

I am...

Introduction

The secret is out![1] There is science to suggest that the law of attraction is real. Quantum mechanics, and the study of the subatomic world has revealed possibilities that range from metaphysical and theoretical to mainstream science. The multiple ways to improve our lives are readily available and, depending on how far down the rabbit hole[2] you wish to go, enlightening. But when it comes to developing the tools necessary for the application of such enlightenment, what the *bleep* do we know?[3]

At about age nine, I began to recognize that there is a connection between what I imagine or think and the manifestation of it in my life. I was unsure for many years if my mind was reading or creating the future, or if I was just a bit crazy. I referred to the experiences at the time as "the magic" or "the knowing." Between 1969 and 1975 I was inspired by such stories as *Horton Hears a Who*[4], *The People*[5], *The Wizard of Oz*[6], and the television show *Bewitched*[7] to contemplate the nature of our existence, our potential and our abilities.

Horton Hears A Who was my introduction to the possibility of infinite universes and perspectives. I read the story at around the same time that I experienced the "Adventure Thru Inner Space" at Disneyland, a ride that simulated a voyage into the world of atoms. The words spoken by the narrator are forever imprinted on my mind, "...I can see that nothing is solid, no matter how it appears."

My fascination with what I called "the magic" or "the knowing" was fueled by the television show *Bewitched* and the television movie *The People*. Both were centered around mystical powers that the characters used. Yet even at a young age, I was a healthy skeptic that held out for proof. I wanted magic, I wanted to believe I had the power to

---

[1] Rhonda Byrne, *The Secret.* Simon & Schuster, Beyond Words Publishing, 2006

[2] *What the Bleep? Down the Rabbit Hole*, DVD, directed by William Arntz, Mark Vicente, Betsy Chasse, Hillsboro: Beyond Words, 2006

[3] *What the Bleep do we Know?*, DVD, directed by William Arntz, Mark Vicente, Betsy Chasse, Los Angeles: Roadside Attractions, 2004

[4] Dr. Suess, *Horton Hears A Who!,* New York: Random House, 1954, film directed by Chuck Jones, Beverly Hills: MGM Animation/Visual Arts, 1970

[5] *The People*, ABC television movie, adapted from a story by Zenna Henderson, directed by John Korty, Los Angeles: American Broadcast Company, 1972

[6] *The Wizard of Oz*, television re-release, directed by Victor Fleming, Beverly Hills: Metro-Goldwyn-Meyer

[7] *Bewitched*, Sol Saks & William Asher, ABC television show, Culver City: Screen Gems, 1971

manifest things in my life, but I wasn't convinced of the possibility. I only wished it to be so.

As a teenager I read and re-read all books from The Hobbit series by J.R.R. Tolkien. The stories took me to a realm that was vivid in my mind. The quest, the magic, the characters all fed my ravenous imagination. There were other books, including the Zenna Henderson series about "The People." Fantasy and science fiction were my escape and my inspiration.

My fascination with the mystery of manifestation continued and became more intense as I grew and expanded my knowledge. In the 1980's I was introduced to quantum mechanics and a hint of the proof I had been looking for. I subscribed to OMNI magazine[8], a science and science fiction fantasy monthly magazine that was instrumental in opening the general public's interest in science. Founded by Kathy Keeton and Bob Guccione, the magazine ran from 1978 to 1995.

The science articles were of interest to me because they were about new theories and exploration of the nature of all things. The articles I read supported my obsession with the interactive nature of existence. That, coupled with years of discussion between me and my father about the theory of evolution and the contrasting views taught in Sunday School, awakened a voracious appetite for more knowledge.

The relevance of this personal disclosure is that to begin any introspective journey we must be ready to let go of what we have been told and trust in what we are inspired to know. We must be willing to open ourselves to all possibilities and look at the world around us in wonder. The healthy balance of skepticism with that openness will keep us in check, but the skeptic must be willing to accept possibilities, and the open part of us must be willing to accept fact.

Once I began to gobble up everything I could find on quantum mechanics and metaphysics, I was immediately thrilled with the reality of the magic. I knew that what I recognized in my life as "the magic" was manifestations of things I desired. It seemed easy and natural. The more complicated life became, however, the more I realized that thoughts really are things and when our thoughts are dark they manifest undesirable things.

Later in my adult life I began to search for a philosophy and community that supported my beliefs. Thus, began the journey of discovering practical tools and activities that would propel me into living in the reality of what I'd always hoped to be true. The

---

[8] OMNI,New York: General Media, Inc., Kathy Keeton & Bob Guccione, 1978-1995,

knowing was real. The magic was real. Now, I simply had to understand how to use it and control it in a way that would benefit my life and the lives of those around me.

This workbook is a result of my experience in manifestation and scripting my life. I am by no means an expert, and I readily admit that this workbook is for the beginner who is not actively engaged in a spiritual practice. The reason for this is purposeful. The practical application of the tools learned through research tends to be the most difficult challenge. It is like anything else that we attempt to change, be it healthy living, mindfulness or other personal improvement activities. It all sounds great, and we feel committed to the program, but the frustration keeps us from a successful outcome.

The first step toward living in the flow of manifestation is to "LIFT" yourself out of the old ways and thoughts. The truth is, it will take some work on your part to change anything. It is, as they say, "an inside job." LIFT is an acronym for:

Love
Inspiration
Forgiveness
Transcendence

Each of the four components will reveal areas of blockage, regret, anger, and self-sabotage. There are four weeks of daily activities that relate to each of the four components.

Love

When I began the process of bringing this book to life, I found myself struggling to get through the first step. I knew that the first step of the LIFT mindset was the most important, love for oneself and others is of course considered the base of a healthy human life. But the question "Do you love yourself?" stopped me in my tracks.

An immediate reaction for one who is on a daily quest of self-improvement and discovery, striving to practice mindful living and express positive interaction is naturally, "Of course I love myself." But how should that feel and how do I know who "myself" is? This question kept me awake for a couple of nights. I could not continue writing this book until I could answer the question. I felt that it had to be answered with authenticity and the highest level of honesty to be shared with others. The dilemma nearly stopped the book from being written because I recognized that I had a long way to go in working on myself before I could possibly consider helping others.

My research turned to another exercise in self-discovery, which involved a return to familiar inspiration and long discussions with family and friends. Much of my own inner work included watching Oprah Winfrey's Super Soul Sunday. [9]

Super Soul Sunday was my weekly dose of mindful medicine. With a variety of guests from authors to actors, teachers to world leaders and every kind of person between, the 60-minute show provided information and thought-provoking ways of improving our lives. It was while watching this show that I heard something that resonated throughout my being.

"WE ALREADY HAVE everything we need. There is no need for self-improvement. All these trips that we lay on ourselves—the heavy-duty fearing that we're bad and hoping that we're good, the identities that we so dearly cling to, the rage, jealousy, and addictions of all kinds—never touch our basic wealth. They are like clouds that temporarily block the sun. But all the time our warmth and brilliance are right here. This is who we really are. We are one blink of an eye away from being fully awake." --Pema Chodron[10]

The immediate recognition of myself was caught in a momentary glimpse just after hearing Pema's words. And though I have read countless books and articles, watched

---

[9] Super Soul Sunday, Harpo Studios & Super Soul Sunday, LLC, Oprah Winfrey Network, 16 October 2011-present

[10] The Pema Chodron Foundation, https://pemachodronfoundation.org/

many videos and talk shows, listened to thousands of spiritual messages, for some reason these words brought forth a feeling, an epiphany. My true self is that quiet, smiling, patient being that resides deep within waiting to be recognized. That being whispers to me often, loves me unconditionally and forgives always.

The next thought that came was the realization that I have been neglectful, abusive and dismissive of my inner being for many years. I felt the same emotion I have experienced after yelling at my children or snapping at my husband, regret and guilt, deep sadness for the way I behaved.

This instant emotional reaction helped me to realize that under all the layers of my perceived self was Me. I thought about the damage I'd done through poor eating and other habits, lack of activity, risky activity, hateful thoughts and self-harm. I thought about all the times I've blamed my body or my hair for how I look or felt anger at my body for illness and disease. The shift of my thinking was instantaneous. I realized that I had caused all the suffering through my irresponsible actions, and then I had blamed my body for all of it.

The moment I envisioned my true self as an innocent being who knows nothing but love, a being that would never hold on to thoughts of anger, hatred or resentment, I shifted. I suddenly knew exactly how it felt to love myself. I reached out to that Me inside, embraced and held her while apologizing, promising to honor her from now on.

I now knew how to feel love for myself. I found unconditional love for that eternal Me, the one who knows everything about me and loves me for it all. The Me who was there before the beginning of this life and the only one who will be there after the end.

Loving yourself is the beginning of all true transformation. It is an acceptance for who you are right now this very moment. Each new moment is a new opportunity to acknowledge yourself again, for with each moment comes a new experience or revelation. I am more than a biological mixture of cells and energy, I have a mind that is in constant action of processing. The processing is involved in my perception of the world around me and my reaction to that world. That reaction is what molds my perception. The perception and the reaction are both under my control. In fact, these are the only things in life that are under my control at all. This understanding helps me to stay connected with my true self because there must be a constant inner dialogue for me to stay in control of my perception and reaction.

The bridge from awareness of my true self to loving my true self is built by recognizing the control I have over my perception and reaction. I must become the guardian for my piece of mind. I must build a filter of truth between what information comes in and how that information is processed. Loving myself begins with protection. This does not mean I protect myself from experiencing emotion, only that I filter out any false information and only allow truth. The truth about any situation may be used for learning and growing, which may lead to a change in perception, but must be viewed as an experience not as shame, guilt, regret or self-doubt.

Shaman and author Don Miguel Ruiz[11] said in the "Four Agreements," "If others say one thing, but do another, you are lying to yourself if you don't listen to their actions. But if you are truthful with yourself, you will save yourself a lot of emotional pain. Telling yourself the truth about it may hurt, but you don't need to be attached to the pain. Healing is on the way, and it's just a matter of time before things will be better for you."

By recognizing the truth in everything we encounter we not only filter out false belief, but we also are able to fully experience the situation and learn from it. When someone is driving very closely behind your car and suddenly passes you and the entire line of cars ahead of you, even though everyone is already at or above the posted speed limit, what is your reaction? The only truth in the situation is that you are driving safely at the posted speed limit, patiently paced at a safe distance behind the person in front of you. The thought in your head that "he isn't following the rules and is being unsafe" may be what you feel and may even be a fact based on the law, but the anger or frustration you experience is your reaction to the thought. Your action is your business. Your reaction is your business. Your perception and thoughts are your business. What he is doing is only your business in determining your perception of safe vs. unsafe, legal vs. illegal, etc. Your reaction can be a fleeting thought of safety or a judgmental assessment of the person. Each reaction will produce a different emotion.

Once we begin to monitor our emotions and determine their relevance to our reaction, then we can begin to change which emotion we allow ourselves to feel. The reaction in the example of a fleeting thought of safety may elicit concern for everyone's safety, empathy and a hope that nothing happens. A reaction of judging the person for his action will elicit anger and resentment. One emotion produces a constructive thought while the other destructive.

As this exercise in analyzing our reaction becomes habit, and we recognize the calm and contented feeling that becomes more frequent, our mindset becomes conditioned to seek out truth and we can control our reactions. This is the first step in loving ourselves.

---

[11] Don Miguel Ruiz, The Four Agreements, Amber-Allen Publishing, July 7 2011

Once this is achieved in our outward interactions, it will lead to our inward interactions. The dialogue we learn to use with others will become the dialogue we use with ourselves. This may seem backward, some may say that we should be able to look into a mirror and see our truth before it will be used outwardly. My experience, however, is that many of us live under layers of self-doubt and self-hatred which manifests as anger toward others. With the practice of looking for truth in our surroundings we learn how to see it in ourselves.

We live in an interactive world. We must learn to observe and experience everything in a meaningful way and process it properly. While yes, transformation is an inside job, it sometimes needs to be triggered from an outside source.

Change how you view the world, how you perceive a situation, how you react to that situation and then recognize the emotions that come up. Know that your reaction and perception is the only thing you have control over.

The second step is to recognize how you keep your temple. Is your body a place to be nurtured, pampered and protected? Is your body a playground for experiencing every pleasure you can find? Is your body a vehicle for all types of thrills? How do you treat your body and mind?

I had to be honest with myself and look back at how I've treated my body. During the process of answering the question "do I love myself?" I discovered that my self-image is directly related to my self-destruction, but not in the obvious way. We already understand that a poor self-image will lead to possible self-destruction but looking deeper I realized that allowing myself to be reckless with my temple damaged it, made it ill. Every time I gazed into a mirror at the dilapidated body before me I cursed it and resented it. The turning point was when I recognized that the body I resented is the body I should have been loving.

The ah-ha moment was when I realized self-hate could only come from seeing a duality of my very self. That my body is the unfortunate victim of its control center. I once thought that my control center is like a computer that receives input and processes it based on experience. Every time the information is processed it creates an established pathway. The image in the mirror is the biological shell I inhabit. If my mind or consciousness is the driver, my body is the car. Though in one way this is somewhat true, that the whole of me is one being wrapped in a material shell. There is no separation, I am the body, mind and energy.

Yes, I realize that this is a simple and common understanding, but in this instance, I was able to make the connection and realize that loving myself meant loving and cherishing the body. It meant recognizing the precious gift of having a body. It is the only body I have for my time on this planet. How am I treating it?

I suddenly felt an overwhelming sense of remorse. I hated my body because I believed it had failed me in my warped sense of perfection, when all the while I was causing the very things I resented. This remorse led to that familiar feeling of a mother who punished her child unjustly or out of anger. A deep sadness and guilt that can be felt all over with a shiver which then settles in the pit of the stomach.

I wanted to hug myself and apologize. In my mind I imagined myself at nine years old, alone and crying, feeling deserted and unloved. I walked to my child self and held her, hugging her tightly and telling her I loved her, telling her how sorry I was for the years of neglect and abuse. I saw my child self as that innocent creative being that was locked up for a very long time and forgotten. This was the true me, waiting to be remembered, waiting to be loved.

My experience may be different from yours, however the point of this is to truly love yourself by recognizing the whole you and feel the emotional connection to that being. Until you feel the emotion, you will not be able to recognize the love. But once you understand the love, you will never be able to forget that part of you again.

Week 1 Activities

- Each morning, when you first look into the mirror, gaze into your own eyes. Continue looking into those eyes for a few moments. Take three cleansing breaths and keep focused on your eyes. Let your breathing be deep and from your diaphragm. Speak to your reflection the following. Repeat it three times.

"I love you and cherish you. I love me and cherish me."

Continue to gaze into your eyes, take one more deep cleansing breath and say, "thank you."

- Each evening look into the mirror before bed, gaze into your own eyes once more. Continue looking silently for a few moments. Take three cleansing breaths and keep focused on your eyes. Breathe deeply from your diaphragm. Speak to your reflection the following. Repeat it three times.

"You are whole, healthy and complete. I am whole, healthy and complete."

Continue to gaze into your eyes, take one more deep cleansing breath and say, "thank you."

At the end of each day, circle how you felt while conducting the activities. Remember, this is only for you, be honest with your feelings.

Day 1:
nothing   uncomfortable   weird   silly   good   calm   content

Day 2:
nothing   uncomfortable   weird   silly   good   calm   content

Day 3
nothing   uncomfortable   weird   silly   good   calm   content

Day 4:
nothing   uncomfortable   weird   silly   good   calm   content

Day 5:
nothing   uncomfortable   weird   silly   good   calm   content

Day 6:
nothing   uncomfortable   weird   silly   good   calm   content

Day 7:
nothing   uncomfortable   weird   silly   good   calm   content

At the end of Day 7, journal your insights and impressions. Explain your feelings and any shifts in them between Day 1 and Day 7.

Journal Page 1

Inspiration

The more I open myself up to daydreaming, imaginary thought and musing, the easier it is to be inspired by the smallest things. The way the morning sun dances through the shadows of the tree branches as it shines through the curtains. Noticing the changing color of the mountains and hills throughout the day. Hearing a bird that reminds me of a camping trip. Simple pleasures that bring a feeling of momentary joy are inspiring and uplifting. It seems that as I experience more of these moments, inspiration comes easier.

But what is inspiration for, and how do we use it? For me, inspiration leads to art, music and writing. My mind is constantly creating future projects. To be honest, there are probably more projects than time available, but completing them is satisfying none the less. Yet, often I have struggled to act on what my mind is holding.

There have been many occasions that I lay awake at night while my mind is busy with ideas, and though I remind myself that I can think more about it the next day, it is sometimes difficult to shut off the racing thoughts. Regardless, without the motivation to start working on a project, or the drive to follow through, many of the ideas just stay in my head like dusty files. It is inspiration that pushes me to bring the ideas to fruition. On days that I am feeling down or doubting my worth, it is challenging to feel inspired. What I have been training myself to do is to listen to certain music, watch an uplifting video, read something positive or take a walk outside and observe nature. The most important thing I've learned is not to force it, but to let it come. If the inspiration doesn't come, or if I do not feel better, I just relax and let it go until the next day.

Inspiration is important because without it we do not move from our safe spot. Those with emotional ups and downs, past trauma and other types of challenges find that staying in the safe spot limits the possibility of failure and disappointment. Yet without taking some risk, we cannot move forward and grow into our full potential. Manifestation for me has been most successful when I move from my safe spot. Inspired activities most often pull me from negative self-talk or thoughts and help put me back in alignment with my strategy for achievement.

I have experienced moments when everything I have asked for is ripe for the taking, and I freeze because I start thinking about the changes, responsibility or obligation that goes with it. These moments have included such things as job opportunities, relationships, relocation, etc. With every opportunity comes change. One way I move from my safe zone and make decisions which necessitate change is to recognize that life always brings change. Even staying put and not moving or growing will not stop change from coming. Nothing is permanent, the world continues to change around me. It is learning to let go of what is familiar or at least allow myself to stop holding so tightly. People, places and things are not forever in our lives...even if we would like them to be. By allowing ourselves to enjoy what is now, and remember life's impermanence, it opens us up to new possibilities and opportunities. Sometimes the decision to stay put for a while is a strategic or necessary choice. It is the emotion or the feeling behind the decision that matters. Was the decision made from fear of change or a recognition that the time is not right? Only you know the truth about that.

Being in the flow of life is all about inspiration and awareness. Being aware of what we are feeling and why, being available for simple beauty to bring a warm feeling and learning to calm ourselves during chaos are just three ways to stay in the flow. There are many others.

Participating in joyful or creative activities raises the level of feel good chemicals, which allow our mind to be more constructive. This is one of the benefits of exercise or taking daily walks, often recommended by doctors for depression. As the blood flow to the brain increases, feel-good chemicals such as dopamine and endorphins are released while chemicals associated with stress are flushed out.[12]

Painting, singing, playing music, even doing the dishes can evoke feelings of calm and encourage inspiration. Some of my greatest ideas come while vacuuming or taking a shower. Remaining open to thoughts and ideas, staying in the moment rather than thinking about the past or ruminating on some experience helps to keep the mind prepped for creativity.

As humans, maintaining a constant state of inspired creativity is something positive to strive for, however there will be moments that interrupt this state. Of course, challenges will come along. It is not that we deny those challenges, it is that we experience them in the moment and then move back to our state of calm and openness as soon as possible. The important thing is to avoid reliving the challenges or imagining a different outcome. Once a thing has happened, it has passed. Accepting what has been and what is, even when difficult, will help to maintain that calmness. Grief, terminal illness and other difficulties are not easy to accept and move on from. Yet, our reactions to those experiences in life are the one thing in our control.

---

[12] The Mayo Clinic
https://www.mayoclinic.org/healthy-lifestyle/stress-management/in-depth/exercise-and-stress/art-20044469

During the most challenging times we may be able to find our greatest creativity. The deepest of emotions elicit inspiration. Some of the most beautiful music and art have been developed from states of despair. Writing poetry, songs or simply journaling about what we are feeling helps to move thoughts from our head and into a tangible place for safekeeping. This is a form of manifestation, moving something from thought to a physical thing. Take that sad or angry thought and create something from it. It is now an object that may be kept or destroyed, but it has been moved from thought to thing under your personal control.

While inspiration is usually considered a moment of uplifting and positive creativity, there are times when we are inspired to do something negative. The important point is that we have the power to use inspiration in whatever way we wish. It is the choice we make that will lead us in one direction or another. How will your inspiration serve you?

Week 2 Activities

- Each morning, the moment you wake up, consider the first thought that comes to you. Evaluate it and look for meaning and cause. Why are you thinking this? As you go about your morning routine, look for signs of nature. Are there birds singing? Is the wind blowing? Is it raining? Can you see sunlight moving through the windows? Take a deep breath, listen closely and pay attention to how you feel about those natural wonders.

- Each evening take a moment to look at the night sky, the moon, the stars or the sunset. Acknowledge the end of the day and everything that has transpired. Imagine all your experiences for the day floating softly into a box. Close the lid of the box and call it complete. Take a deep breath and move away from the day which has passed. Speak these words:

"Today is at rest, tomorrow is a new beginning."

Tell yourself "thank you" for allowing inspired moments and staying in the flow.

At the end of each day, circle how you felt while conducting the activities. Remember, this is only for you, be honest with your feelings.

Day 1:
nothing   uncomfortable   weird   silly   good   calm   content

Day 2:
nothing   uncomfortable   weird   silly   good   calm   content

Day 3
nothing   uncomfortable   weird   silly   good   calm   content

Day 4:
nothing   uncomfortable   weird   silly   good   calm   content

Day 5:
nothing   uncomfortable   weird   silly   good   calm   content

Day 6:
nothing   uncomfortable   weird   silly   good   calm   content

Day 7:
nothing   uncomfortable   weird   silly   good   calm   content

At the end of Day 7, journal your insights and impressions. Explain your feelings and any shifts in them between Day 1 and Day 7.

Journal Page 2

Forgiveness

It is widely known that forgiveness can ease a troubled mind, but it is also known to improve mental and physical health. According to the American Psychology Association, "Whether you've suffered a minor slight or a major grievance, learning to forgive those who hurt you can significantly improve both psychological well-being and physical health." [13]

For years we have known that stress is damaging to our body. Imagine how much anger, resentment, and thoughts of revenge increase that stress. Holding onto negative feelings and reliving past negative experiences fire the same areas of the brain as the actual event. When we learn to forgive, we learn how to shift the emotion of resentment, regret, anger, and shame.

Forgiveness is not about forgetting, it is about acknowledgment of the thing that happened, allowing an emotional response, then moving from the emotional response to a place of truth and observance. Observe the thing that happened from afar, without emotional attachment to it. Consider all the factors and players, examine the truth about them. Sit with the pain, but let it subside. Holding on to the pain and reliving the thing that happened is like sinking further into a mudhole, while ignoring the ladder next to you that will lead you out. We choose to stay in pain, and though for some it is more difficult than others, at some point we must move away from the pain to continue forward.

It is not only important to forgive others, it is equally important to forgive oneself. This may be the second most difficult challenge in becoming whole. The layers of guilt, regret, shame and insecurity we have allowed ourselves to absorb are not easy to shake off. I still struggle with this one from time to time. It is closely linked to loving myself, because if I cannot forgive myself it is difficult to love myself. Yet, we assume that we are alone in having made mistakes or been dishonest or cruel. We can try to justify many things, but deep inside we know our own truth. That truth is important to admit. Until you admit your part in something undesirable, you will continue to lie to yourself about it and not experience forgiveness. When we cannot forgive ourselves, it will lead us to find fault with others, and be less forgiving.

---

[13] Wier, Kristin, 2017. Forgiveness can improve physical and mental health, American Psychological Association.
https://www.apa.org/monitor/2017/01/ce-corner, accessed June 2020.

When a thing is horrific, traumatic, and life altering, it becomes a monster that grows as we feed it with our fear and remorse. Night terrors, sudden emotional outbursts, racing or lingering thoughts are all part of post-traumatic stress. We have seen many stories of families struck by violence and the loss of a loved one, who show kindness and forgiveness toward the person responsible for the tragedy. These are people who understand that there is no peace for them while harboring resentment for another. Honoring their loved one is best done by loving and forgiving. This does not mean forgoing justice, but it does not leave room for vengeful justice either. The consequences of an action, cause and effect, are the true law of nature. We can choose to trap ourselves in the past with the action or move forward with the consequences and use them as a force for good in our lives.

Forgiveness may be as simple as feeling love for the lady who cuts you off while driving on the highway, or as challenging as saying a prayer for the person who killed your loved one. As humans we are bound to one another in a state of interaction, and each choice will influence someone else. The choices we make can start a positive chain of like reactions, or a negative chain. Both will exponentially increase, but the positive chain reaction explodes in light and a powerful vibration of love, while the negative explodes in dark and brings everything down into despair. Which is best for our health and overall life experience? The choice seems obvious, though not always easy.

It takes some work to move to a natural state of gratitude and forgiveness, especially when we have learned to live in a state of fear, guilt, resentment, and regret. Like any other habit we would like to expel from our lives, the habit of reacting out of guilt and resentment may be eliminated if we make mindful choices.

I have worked through the forgiveness stage and found it challenging, especially to forgive myself. Yet, in the process of understanding why it is important, and slipping often, I have been able to forgive myself for the slips, which helped me feel the emotion of forgiveness and step away enough to be okay with starting again. As they say in the twelve-step programs, "One day at a time." Sometimes it is one moment at a time.

What does it feel like to forgive yourself? When you raise your voice at someone, and realize that it is because you are frustrated or tired, do you apologize and try to do better? If someone does the same to you, are you able to forgive that person?

Week 3 Activities

Each morning, the moment you wake up, check your mood. Do you feel good, ready to take on the day? Or are you resentful and thinking about all the things that make you angry? If your first thought is of something negative, try to step away from it and look at it logically. Make the effort to remove any emotional tie with the thought. Look at the facts of it, be thankful for the experience or the person in expectation of a lesson or a growth opportunity. Remind yourself that challenges are chances for change and growth.

Each evening think about anyone or anything that may have challenged your mood. Before going to bed, be sure to find something positive about that person, thing or situation. Envision that positive thought expanding and changing into a beautiful bubble of light. As the bubble grows, it floats away from you to move into its own space. Allow it to go, feel kindness toward it. Before closing your eyes to sleep, say these words:

"All is one, the love in me recognizes the love in you."

Tell yourself "thank you" for the forgiveness of yourself and others.

At the end of each day, circle how you felt while conducting the activities. Remember, this is only for you, be honest with your feelings.

Day 1:
nothing   uncomfortable   weird   silly   good   calm   content

Day 2:
nothing   uncomfortable   weird   silly   good   calm   content

Day 3
nothing   uncomfortable   weird   silly   good   calm   content

Day 4:
nothing   uncomfortable   weird   silly   good   calm   content

Day 5:
nothing   uncomfortable   weird   silly   good   calm   content

Day 6:
nothing   uncomfortable   weird   silly   good   calm   content

Day 7:
nothing   uncomfortable   weird   silly   good   calm   content

At the end of Day 7, journal your insights and impressions. Explain your feelings and any shifts in them between Day 1 and Day 7.

Journal Page 3

Transcendence

There are many ways that we understand transcendence. Human psychological transcendence is said to be a state of the highest consciousness in behavior and deed in relating to all forms of life. Spiritual transcendence is explained as a human perception of an experience of the sacred, that influences one's self perception and relations. To transcend is to rise above, this can be expressed by a parent advising a child to ignore hateful words as in "rise above it, ignore it." But it also may be expressed as a person in a fearful situation surrendering and finding momentary peace. It is an act of separating oneself from the actual event, looking at it from outside and choosing how to react. Rising above would be the act of acknowledging the fear or despair and then moving to a state of observance versus attachment.

To transcend the emotional attachment is not to become inhuman, it is to become fully human. As mindfulness becomes our normal process for interacting with the world, we tap into the abilities that are thought to be unique in human consciousness. The innate fight or flight responses that are built into our nervous system, may be overridden by mindful attention to the reality of a situation. Rising above in this sense is taking a breath to analyze the whole picture.

Transcendence is experienced when we consciously choose how to react and can calmly move through an experience without emotion or ego interfering with that choice. Defensive driver courses teach drivers to respond to road hazards with well-focused, calm and practiced maneuvers. This type of training helps a driver to avoid emotional response, overcorrecting or panic which may, in turn, avoid tragic accidents. Learning to transcend above our emotional response is similar in its advantages. It is also similar in the necessity for training and practice.

Practicing transcendence daily helps it to become a natural state of being. Transcending above it all does not mean being better than or above anything in a hierarchical sense, it refers to our removing ourselves from the emotional reactive attachment to the thing itself. When a person says something hurtful to me, I can either react and be angry, ignore it, or acknowledge it and walk away from it. Inside, my emotional attachment to the incident is what really matters. The quicker I can look at the truth in it and move away, the easier it is to retain my inner peace.

Painful or fearful situations can be made much less stressful when we are trained to transcend them. Knowing that each moment is precious, holding our peace and allowing the challenge to pass without losing control helps to keep our mind alert and able to make healthy decisions. Decisions made in haste during panic do not always serve us best. This is not to say we wait to get out of the way of a vehicle or when avoiding an object, however, training ourselves to stay calm in every situation will help us to become conditioned to split second decisions that are made based on calm and rational thought.

The most important meaning in transcendence is to rise above the minutia. The petty things that we spend too much time noticing. Gossip, rumors, false information, negative self-talk are all things that we must rise above. They do not serve us, so we are best not to spend our energy or time paying attention to them. We can speak up when it is appropriate, but only with fact, love and a sense of finding solutions. Otherwise, we will be wallowing in the mud with negative emotional attachment to untruths.

Transcendence is a learned behavior, one that I work on every day. Being the type of person who has always jumped on the soap box for one crusade after another, I can be easily lost in the swirling pool of petty debate. I must be reminded that example is the best form of influence. It is in the delivery of the message that much more is heard. A seed rarely sprouts when it is forced into dry, hard ground without any nurturing. Further, without hearing all sides of an issue or all remedies suggested for a problem, we are blind to the potential truth coming from an unexpected place. Rising above and leaving the ego behind allows one to be open to all possibilities. This is my most difficult task, as my ego tries to lead me believe that only my ideas are the most effective.

As we begin to learn more about ourselves and the reasons we react to the things we do in the way we do, we will find a longing for a better way. It becomes far more comfortable to let the little things go and calmly engage the big things once we have practiced mindful transcendence. Consider your reactions to situations. Consider what triggers you to anger. What might it feel like to rise above it and watch yourself react without control?

Week 4 Activities

- Each morning, the moment you wake up, sit comfortably in a quiet space, close your eyes and imagine that you are floating above yourself and your day, watching it all play out. See a problem or situation that you may have some apprehension about and watch it happen from overhead. Watch yourself calmly handle it with confidence and love. Smile to yourself as you imagine you are your own puppet master, consciously causing the situation to play out as a win-win, or with a beneficial ending.
- Each evening think back over your day and make a mental list of all the moments you consciously intervened with your ego or emotional reaction and transcended above it. Feel the calm that you were able to generate. Know that even if you were not able to completely give over to the transcendental self, your intention was there. Say these words:

"I know that I am the me that guides me."

Tell yourself "thank you" for the efforts of the week.

At the end of each day, circle how you felt while conducting the activities. Remember, this is only for you, be honest with your feelings.

Day 1:
nothing   uncomfortable   weird   silly   good   calm   content

Day 2:
nothing   uncomfortable   weird   silly   good   calm   content

Day 3
nothing   uncomfortable   weird   silly   good   calm   content

Day 4:
nothing   uncomfortable   weird   silly   good   calm   content

Day 5:
nothing   uncomfortable   weird   silly   good   calm   content

Day 6:
nothing   uncomfortable   weird   silly   good   calm   content

Day 7:
nothing   uncomfortable   weird   silly   good   calm   content

At the end of Day 7, journal your insights and impressions. Explain your feelings and any shifts in them between Day 1 and Day 7.

Journal Page 4

Congratulations!

You have completed four weeks of inner work. This is a wonderful thing you have accomplished. Do something loving for yourself. Remember that, we are always growing and expanding our awareness, the learning does not end. Maintaining what we have learned ingrains it into our natural way of being.

Loving yourself....

You have processed through how you relate to YOU. You recognize the unique being that you are and have learned how to love that being.

Inspiration....

You have learned to find inspiration in the smallest of things. Your creativity will blossom the more you seek that state of inspired action.

Forgiveness....

You have learned that forgiving others is necessary for being your best, and that before you can forgive others, you must first forgive yourself.

Transcendence....

You have learned to transcend the minutia of drama and negative talk, and to rise above the emotional to look upon the truth.

Now go and be your best you!

Insights

Record your discoveries here, remind yourself of why you decided to read this workbook and complete the activities.

What surprised you?

What did you already know?

Have you changed anything in your daily habits? If yes, What?

What is your greatest challenge? How will you manage that?

 About the author….

Cheryl Ann Hunter is a southern California mother of four, grandmother of three. She and her husband Mike reside in Desert Hot Springs with their two cats.

Visit Cheryl's website www.cherylannhunter.com
to experience more of the author's writing and discover her artwork.

A message from the author:

Dear reader,

It is my hope that you have found something useful from this book. I have been working on improving my mindset for many years, and the words contained in this workbook are a result of that quest.

As of the publishing of this book in June of 2020, the world has been in a chaotic state. With a pandemic internationally, racism and violence in the United States, and an uncertain future for so many, I feel compelled to write about ways that we can all improve.

Our future is only as bright and promising as we humans are willing to make it. By making the effort to improve our own little corner of the world, we are creating a positive wave of influence that will grow exponentially.

Be good to yourself and others, that is the one thing we all can do.

Other works by Cheryl Ann Hunter available on Amazon

Bun-Bun's Theory of Everything
Paperback: 44 pages
Publisher:CreateSpace
Independent
Publishing Platform;
2nd edition (July 11, 2014)
Language: English
ISBN-10: 1508578400
ISBN-13:978-1508578406
Product Dimensions:
6.7 x 0.1 x 9.6 inches

Bottle or Breast? Only Mom Knows Best!
Paperback: 44 pages
Publisher: Independent
(June 9, 2020)
Language: English
ISBN-13:979-8652384043
ASIN: B089TWSBFR
Product Dimensions:
6 x 0.1 x 9 inches

Yucaipa and My White Privilege
Paperback: 48 pages
Publisher: Independently
published (June 20, 2020)
Language: English
ISBN-13: 979-8655484337
ASIN: B08BF14JYJ Product
Dimensions:
6 x 0.1 x 9 inches